Future Stars of America 2

By

Ron Berman

www.scobre.com

Scobre Press Corporation
2255 Calle Clara
La Jolla, CA 92037

Scobre Press books may be purchased for
educational, business or sales promotional use.

First Scobre edition published 2006.

"The Dream Series"

Edited by Helen Glenn Court
Cover Art & Layout by Michael Lynch

ISBN # 1-933423-51-X

HOME RUN EDITION
These stories are based on real life, although some names,
quotes, and details of events have been slightly altered.

www.scobre.com

SCOBRE PRESS
The Athletes Behind the Action

Future Stars of America 2

Table of Contents

Clay Marzo of Hawaii, is surrounded
by fans during an interview.

Photo courtesy of Tom Cozad

Hawaii's Local Treasure

Dawn Patrol

As the sun began to rise over the ocean, water splashed against Clay Marzo's face. He and his older brother paddled out for their first ride of the day. The only other people in the ocean were a couple of local surfers. They smiled and nodded to Clay. Everyone knows the sixteen-year-old superstar. After all, Clay has been surfing these waters for most of his life.

Clay was out on dawn patrol. That means he was in the water very early in the morning. Clay knows of an out-of-the-way spot called the Pool. It's the perfect place to surf at dawn, when the sun is just coming up.

Clay lives in a town called Lahaina [pronounced lah-high-nah]. It's located on the island of Maui, in the beautiful state of Hawaii. "My family moved to Hawaii from San Diego when I was a baby," Clay explains. "I can never thank my parents enough for bringing me to this amazing spot." He isn't kidding. Lahaina has awesome waterfalls and friendly people.

Clay had woken up at five o'clock in the morning. It was quiet and dark. At that hour, most people on the island were fast asleep. It was tough getting out of bed so early, but Clay wanted to surf. After getting dressed, he had gulped down some cereal and juice. Then he and his brother grabbed their surfboards. In

1

a flash, they were out the door and on the way to the ocean.

On a typical day, Clay will surf for several hours. It's easy because he lives close to the ocean. He can even smell the salt air through the open windows of his house. That always makes him think about surfing. There's nothing Clay loves more than being out in the water.

Clay knows how lucky he is to be raised in Hawaii. "Sometimes I can't believe I live in the best place on earth," he says. "When I travel to other countries to surf, it's awesome, of course. But there's nothing quite like the feeling of being home in Lahaina."

Surfing Baby

Clay Marzo was born with surfing in his blood. His mom was a surfer, and his Aunt Shelly was a junior champion. That's not all. His grandmother still surfs! Growing up, it also helped to have an older brother to look up to. Clay's brother is a great surfer.

Even as a baby, Clay was drawn to the water. By the time he was two, he was already surfing—sort of. His father would go out surfing, and Clay would tag along.

As his father paddled out, two-year-old Clay would sit on the nose of the surfboard. He had a fun way of passing the time while his father waited for a good wave. He enjoyed jumping off the surfboard as if it were a diving board. He would splash around in the water before climbing right back on. When a wave came along, Clay would hang on, screaming with joy.

When Clay was five years old, he entered his first surfing competition. It had divisions for kids of all ages. When he easily won the contest, people took notice of him.

As the years passed, Clay continued to surf. By the time he was ten, he was already becoming well known. He traveled to California, where the National Championships were being held. Clay competed against the best surfers in the world in his age group. Although this was his first time in a big contest, he placed third. People who watched him were impressed. They all said that Clay Marzo was going to be a famous surfer one day.

Hanging out with Kelly

"Kelly? He's just awesome, what can I say?" You can hear the respect in Clay's voice. He was recently given an opportunity that most surfers can only dream about. Clay got to surf with the best surfer in the world—Kelly Slater.

Slater has achieved many things. He captured his first title in 1992 at the age of twenty. That made him the youngest world champion ever, but it was only the beginning. He went on to win a record six world titles. He took the sport of surfing to a whole new level.

For Clay, the chance to surf with Kelly Slater

sounded like a crazy dream. He wondered if one of his friends was playing a practical joke on him. But, no, it was true. The company Quiksilver invited Clay to go on a surfing trip. Soon he and ten other young surfers were on a huge boat. They were traveling to the country of Indonesia with Kelly Slater.

When Clay talks about his journey, his bright blue eyes light up. "Dude, the boat had its own personal chef, a helicopter pad, DVD players in every room, personal bathrobes . . . I felt like the king of a country or something!" Of course, the best part was that Kelly was there. Clay and the other surfers hung out with him the whole time. "We all learned so much just by being with Kelly," Clay explains.

When Kelly wasn't in the water with the young surfers, he taught them many things. He also told them about his incredible surfing adventures all around the world. Clay loved hearing these stories. They made him want to improve as a surfer and be like Kelly.

Unique Bond

When sixteen-year-old Clay Marzo isn't in the ocean, he has many other things going on. One of his hobbies is swimming. But Clay isn't just out there splashing around for fun. He happens to be a talented swimmer. Two years ago, he won the state championship in the 200 freestyle event. Clay was also a member of his high school swim team one year. His coach had great praise for him. "Clay has the instinct of an Olympic swimmer," he said. "I sure wish I could get him to swim full time."

Clay also likes working with computers. He has an interest in shooting and editing videos. Naturally, the main thing he shoots is surfing action. He films his friends as they surf. Then they film him when he's ripping it out in the water. When Clay gets home, he edits the surfing footage. He adds things to make it look like a professional video. He uses music, slow motion, and all kinds of cool tricks to add flavor.

Creating videos is a difficult process. But Clay is completely focused when he's doing something he enjoys. Once he's satisfied with the finished product, he'll e-mail it to his friends. They are always blown away. It's an added bonus that this hobby helps him with his surfing. "When I see myself out there, I can sometimes spot ways that I can improve. Or I'll notice things that I did wrong," Clay explains.

Clay has a lot of hobbies, and all of them seem to involve the water. It's obvious that there's a unique bond between Clay and the ocean—he's connected to it in a very deep way. But that's not even the most important thing. His parents are vrey proud that he's a polite and easygoing kid. Clay has a big smile and an even bigger heart. That's probably why he's so popular back home in Lahaina. This beautiful island has many local treasures. Among them is a cool kid who is also a surfing champion—Clay Marzo.

Perfect 10

When the airplane touched down, Clay looked over at his father with a wide grin. He always enjoys competing against other great surfers. He had recently been named "King of the Camp" at Camp Hobgood. That's a camp for some of the best young surfers in the world. Of course, there had also been the trip with Kelly Slater. So the year was off to a promising start. It was about to get even better.

Once again, Clay was headed to California for the National Championships. Every surfer in the country would be trying to beat him. But none of that was going to matter. Clay Marzo was about to become a superstar.

A week later, Clay hit the beach for the last round of the competition. He was ready for an intense day of surfing. He had advanced to the finals with ease. Today would be a true test, though. The contest had come down to the four best surfers. Each one was a champion. Not only that, but all of them were older. They were surfers with more experience than Clay.

Clay gazed out at the ocean with a look of excitement on his face. The weather was spectacular, with only a slight wind blowing. The waves were five to six feet. These were perfect conditions. Clay waxed up his board and stretched. Meanwhile, friends were coming up to him to talk and to wish him good luck.

The competition got under way. The fans on the beach were treated to some awesome surfing action. The surfers were putting on quite a show. Late in the contest, it had come down to just two competitors—Clay Marzo and Torrey Meister.

Clay had already pulled off the near-impossible—a perfect 10 on one of his rides. Still, he was behind in the overall score. The contest rules were that the best two scores a surfer received were added together. The surfer with the higher score would be declared the winner at the end. Torrey had scored a 9 and an 8, so he had a combined score of 17. Besides his 10, the best Clay had scored was a 6. So he was trailing by a full point. He needed an 8 or better to win.

Clay rode a couple of waves, but without any real success. Time was starting to run out. Suddenly, he spotted a large wave coming right at him. Clay began paddling to get into position. Dipping deep into the barrel, he shot out with speed. He finished with a huge air-reverse. The crowd on the beach went crazy! This was the sweetest thing they had seen all day. Everyone turned to the judges to see what score they would award.

Clay heard a loud roar coming from the crowd. He couldn't believe it when he saw his score posted. The judges had given him another perfect 10! No one had ever achieved two perfect scores in the finals. The contest was over. The fans on the beach were cheering loudly for Clay.

Smiling brightly, Clay held up his shiny trophy.

Clay's room at his home in Lahaina.
Check out all those trophies!

Just chillin' in the clear blue
water of the Pacific Ocean.

He felt very satisfied. He doesn't surf for money or fame. He surfs because the ocean is where he *needs* to be. One way or another, Clay is always going to be connected to the ocean. As long as he's in the water, Clay will always be scoring a perfect 10. That's because Clay Marzo is a special guy, a talented surfer . . . and a future star of America!

Ritchie Guerrero of Arizona,
is on his way to being number one!

FUTURE WORLD CHAMP

Baby Ritchie was born to box.

Born to Box

Inspiration

Sweat dripped down Ritchie Guerrero's fore-head. It gathered in a small puddle on the ground beneath his feet. Ritchie didn't even notice that there was a cut above his right eye. A couple of small drops of blood dripped from it. The cut had come when the huge punching bag scraped against the side of his face.

Tonight, Ritchie was the only person in the gym. It was very quiet. The only noise was the sound of Ritchie hitting the punching bag. It was late, and every other boxer had gone home. Ritchie, however, *was* home. He was at the Tigers Boxing Club. This gym was owned by his parents and located right next door to his house. That was perfect for Ritchie. It allowed him to train longer and harder than most boxers his age.

Ritchie had been there for three hours already. At the moment, he was giving the punching bag a fierce beating. *Whap!* A quick jab to create a little space. *Thwack!* A sharp blow to the body. *Crunch!* Ritchie hit the bag as hard as he could. It felt like he could almost punch right through it.

Ritchie started to feel a little tired. The fifteen-year-old boxer thought about stopping. Reaching for a water bottle, he looked over to the wall by the locker room. A large American flag hung there. Below it was a photo of his hero, Oscar De la Hoya.

Next to the photo of De la Hoya was a copy of an Olympic gold medal. Ritchie stares at it sometimes. He can almost imagine that it's a *real* gold medal. In these moments, he pictures the national anthem playing loudly. He pictures the gold medal being placed around his neck.

Inspired, Ritchie quickly began punching the bag again. He wasn't ready to quit for the night. He couldn't stop training until he put in a little bit more work. As always, his determination was giving him energy.

It was eleven o'clock in the evening. A lot of people in his neighborhood were already in bed. Not Ritchie. There was a reason he was putting in this extra time at the gym. He needed it after a poor performance in a recent boxing match. Sure, he could have gone over to Bobby's house. The guys were eating pizza and watching a DVD. But Ritchie was here, alone at the gym on a Friday night. He wasn't hanging out with his friends. Instead, he was working on his jabbing and punching.

That's the kind of dedication Ritchie Guerrero has. He knows that these sacrifices are important. That's what it takes to be a fighter.

That's what it takes to become a champion.

The Tigers Boxing Club
Even as a young kid, Ritchie Guerrero loved

boxing. His dad had been an amateur fighter. He would tell Ritchie exciting stories about famous boxing matches. Ritchie, who is half Mexican, has always idolized Oscar De la Hoya. He wants to follow in De la Hoya's footsteps and become a champion.

To give Ritchie a chance to achieve his goals, his parents have made a lot of sacrifices. One of them happened when Ritchie was only ten years old. It had a big impact on his boxing career. Mr. and Mrs. Guerrero decided to move their family to Arizona. They bought a small house that had an empty lot next to it. They felt this would be a great place for their children to grow up.

At first, the lot next to their new house remained empty. Then, one night Mr. and Mrs. Guerrero had a serious talk. Boxing was in their blood. They had always dreamed of building their very own boxing gym. They wanted it to be a place where kids could do something fun. That would be better than just hanging out and getting into trouble. It would also help Ritchie, who was developing into a fine young boxer.

Mr. and Mrs. Guerrero made their decision. They built the Tigers Boxing Club. It immediately became popular in the neighborhood. Mrs. Guerrero says, "It makes us proud that kids now have a place they can go. It's healthy for them, it's fun, and it keeps them out of trouble. Some of the kids have become excellent fighters, too."

Everyone agrees that Ritchie is the best fighter

at the Tigers Boxing Club. He has always been determined to become a champion. Even back at the ages of eleven and twelve, his results in the ring were fantastic. People started to realize that Ritchie was someone to keep an eye on.

Knock-Down

When Ritchie was twelve, he received an important boxing lesson. He was fighting Sammy Nelson, a tough opponent. Twelve-year-old Sammy was taller than Ritchie. He also outweighed him by twenty pounds. But that didn't matter. Ritchie's skill and footwork were very advanced. He was landing some powerful combinations. In this three-round bout, Ritchie won the first two rounds. He seemed to be on his way to another victory.

Twenty seconds into the final round, something happened to Ritchie that had never happened before. He had gone straight to Sammy's body. After landing a left hook, Ritchie had followed with a huge right uppercut. Unfortunately, he also left himself wide open. This was Sammy's chance. He came in with a straight jab. Then he put the full weight of his body behind his fearsome right hand—and connected with an uppercut to Ritchie's face. The crowd was stunned when Ritchie went down.

"It felt like I had run into a solid brick wall," Ritchie remembers. "I learned that you have to make sure you're protected at all times."

For the first time in his life, Ritchie found himself on the canvas. The referee, standing over him, was counting. "One, two, three . . ." Ritchie was dazed at first. For a second, he wasn't sure what was happening. "Four, five, six . . ." then suddenly he remembered what was going on. He wasn't going down *that* easily. "Seven, eight . . ." suddenly, Ritchie jumped to his feet as the crowd exploded with cheers. The referee looked him over and held up his hand. He signaled that the match could continue.

Ritchie had been cut on the corner of his mouth. That made him even more determined. Over the next sixty seconds, he went on the attack. Using his left-right combination, he pounded Sammy. He landed several punches, including a jarring uppercut.

The bell rang, signaling the end of the fight. This was a good thing, because otherwise the referee would have stopped the fight. That's how much Ritchie was hurting his opponent. It didn't matter that he had been knocked down. He had responded with the heart of a champion. Ritchie's comeback had made him the winner of the round—and the fight.

"I learned many things that day," Ritchie explains. "My parents always tell me that you get knocked down in life. But you have to get back up again." He laughs and says, "This time I *really* got knocked down—on my butt, on the canvas! But I got up again, and that felt good. Life is all about picking yourself up and making your way through difficult stuff."

Going for the Gold

"Monday through Friday, at least four hours a day." Ritchie isn't talking about his school schedule. He's talking about his training schedule. Most people don't realize that successful boxers have to train extremely long hours. Ritchie has a routine that begins right when he gets home from school. After eating a snack, he gets to work. And he works *very* hard.

A typical training session begins with jump roping. This helps with footwork and coordination. Then Ritchie puts on the "wraps." This is the white tape that fighters wear to protect their hands from blisters.

At the Tigers Boxing Club, there are three heavy punching bags. Each one is a different size. Ritchie trains in sets of three minutes. That's the length of a boxing round. He'll practice his punching and jabbing on the first bag for three or four rounds. Then he moves on to the next punching bag. He will do three or four more rounds, and then move to the last bag. There, he does three or four *more* rounds.

After resting for a moment and drinking some water, Ritchie continues. He moves on to the next part of his training—dodge ball. Actually, it's a version of that game. There's a huge bag filled with sand that hangs from the ceiling. Ritchie and his dad give the heavy bag a big push. This causes it to start moving around quickly. Ritchie stands in the way of the bag as if it's another boxer. But instead of throwing punches, he practices dodging the bag.

This is an important part of the training session. The bag moves fast and is very heavy, so dodging it isn't easy. Ritchie explains why this matters so much: "A boxer is always switching from offense to defense. That's one of the things that make boxing an exciting sport. Sometimes the best part of a boxing match isn't the punch a guy throws. It's how he gets out of the way of another guy's punch."

When he's done with that, Ritchie does push-ups and sit-ups—at least a hundred of each. Then he goes outside. There are steep hills near his house. Ritchie runs up and down. He keeps going until he can't run any more. Sometimes, instead of running, he has a sparring match. Sparring is a practice boxing match.

All of this effort has paid off for fifteen-year-old Ritchie Guerrero. He's come a long way. It's been years since he was knocked down by Sammy Nelson. Since then, Ritchie has accomplished many cool things. One of them happened at the Ringside World Championship. Ritchie went up against some of the best young fighters in the world. Displaying his talent, he made it all the way to the final round.

With his confidence growing, Ritchie then went to the Arizona Junior Olympics. He crushed the competition, winning the whole thing. That was one of the thrills of his life. It motivated him for another

Olympics. In 2008, Ritchie will be eighteen years old—and ready for the *real* Olympics, which will be held in China.

Ritchie is ready for his next opponent.

When asked about his dream, Ritchie shrugs his shoulder. He smiles and says, "I'm going for gold." The Olympics are the highest goal an amateur athlete can shoot for. Ritchie is trying to follow in the footsteps of his hero, Oscar De la Hoya.

Nobody knows what will end up happening in Ritchie's boxing career. No matter what, he's determined to go to college. He's interested in business, and he wants to get a good education. Ritchie is thinking about combining his love of boxing with his good business sense. What does this mean? Well, maybe a Ritchie Guerrero Boxing Club!

Wherever life leads Ritchie, he won't be far away from boxing. He loves the sound of a heavy bag being pounded. He is used to seeing a jump rope moving quickly through the air. After all, he was born to box—and born to be a future star of America!

Jayme Jarvis of California,
stands tall with her bat in hand.

A Fitting Tribute

Disappointment

Thirteen-year-old Jayme Jarvis stared out at the empty softball diamond. She felt sad, angry, and disappointed. Ten minutes had passed since the final out of the game. Jayme still wasn't ready to walk off the field, though. It was hard to believe that the season was over. After a few more minutes, she finally joined her teammates in the dugout.

The dugout was pretty quiet. Jayme took a seat in the corner. Coach Douglas was telling everyone that it was a great season. But all Jayme could think was: *How could we have missed the playoffs*? Had it been crazy to think that the East County Red Team could reach the nationals? Would they ever get there?

These were important issues because softball is a big part of Jayme's life. She got her start when she was only four years old. Her mom used to let her swing a wooden bat off a tee. As the years passed, Jayme improved quickly. She played all the time, working on her fielding and practicing her powerful swing.

Things really started to get serious when Jayme was twelve. She became a member of the prestigious East County Red Team. The other girls accepted Jayme almost immediately. They saw that she shared their passion for the game. Together, they had dreams of winning a national title.

But today it had all ended suddenly. After Coach Douglas finished speaking, Jayme and her teammates remained in the dugout. Jayme looked at her friends and said, "Coach is trying to make us all feel good. He's telling us that the season was a success. Well, in some ways it *was* a great season. I mean, we sure had a lot of fun. But the bottom line is simple: we weren't good enough. Every one of us needs to get better so next season we *are* good enough."

The girls all nodded their heads in agreement. They put their hands into the middle of a circle. They promised each other that they would spend the off-season working harder than ever. This moment was a turning point for the East County Red Team. It would pay off for them in a big way.

All-Star

The Red Team was trailing 6-4 going into the last inning. The fans in the stands were clapping and stamping their feet. With the heart of the order due up, there was still hope. The Red Team always seemed to get clutch hits when they needed them. This was one of the reasons they had a fantastic record. They were 36 and 4 coming into today's game.

On the first day of training camp, Coach Douglas had been amazed. Jayme and the other girls had kept their promise. They had come back bigger, stronger, and faster. Coach Douglas knew that this was going to be a special year.

For Jayme, this had turned into a great season. It was capped off by making the League All-Star Team. That showed how much she was improving. But the real satisfaction came from the performance of the squad. The Red Team played in tournaments weekend after weekend. At one point they won five consecutive tournaments. That added up to a total of *thirty* games in a row.

With one out and Lauren on first, Megan slapped a single to right. Joanne then flied out to left field. The Red Team was now down to its final out. As Jayme loosened up in the on-deck circle, Amber stepped to the plate. She ripped the first pitch sharply into left field. With Lauren wisely stopping at third, the bases were loaded.

Jayme took her practice swings. Meanwhile, the manager of the opposing team came out of the dugout. She wanted to talk with her pitcher. "Jayme is leading the league in home runs," the manager said. "Let's not give her anything good to hit. We'd be better off to walk in a run and take our chances on the next batter. Keep everything down and away."

Following instructions, the pitcher threw the first two balls out of the strike zone. Jayme moved closer to the plate. With a 2 and 0 count, the pitcher went into her windup. Once again, the pitch was low and away—but Jayme was ready this time. She hit a sizzling grounder up the first base line. With the crowd roaring from the stands, Lauren and Megan scored easily. Amber was running down the line. She was going to try and score to win the game!

With the crowd on its feet, Amber slid sharply into home plate. Her slide created a huge cloud of dust. The umpire shouted, "Safe!" The fans exploded. The East County Red Team had won the game. This was their thirty-seventh victory. They definitely weren't missing the playoffs this year. In fact, their dream of reaching the nationals was getting even closer.

Family Tragedy

A month later, Jayme woke up suddenly from a restless sleep. As she got out of bed, she thought, *something is wrong.* She glanced outside and noticed that the weather was very cloudy.

Jayme and the girls were in a hotel in a small town in California. It was about fifty miles from Jayme's home in Spring Valley. The East County Red Team was participating in an important tournament. The winning team would be awarded the prize of a trip to the nationals.

After winning their first two games, the Red Team had reached the semifinals. They had an evening game that was beginning at seven thirty. As always, Jayme hung out with Amber, Lauren, and the rest of the team. For some reason, though, she wasn't in a cheerful mood. When her mom got a phone call, Jayme asked, "What's going on, Mom?"

Mrs. Jarvis didn't want to worry her daughter

before a big game. "Alida had to go to the hospital," she answered. "I'm sure it's nothing to be concerned about. She just has a bad fever. You stay here with the team and I'll head over to the hospital."

Alida Grace Millum was Jayme's cousin. She was also one of the joys of Jayme's life. This beautiful baby was only two years old. She had already brought a lot of laughter and happiness into the family.

At first Jayme tried to tell herself that there was nothing to worry about. It was a Saturday, so the doctor's office was closed. The hospital would be the only place to go if a baby was sick. This didn't mean anything terrible. Jayme, however, had a weird feeling.

At seven o'clock, the team headed over to the field. Once again, a strange feeling came over Jayme. Borrowing a cell phone, she quickly called her house. Her father answered. Jayme sensed that something had happened. "Dad, is . . . is Alida okay?"

"Jayme," Mr. Jarvis said softly, "isn't your game about to start?"

"Yeah, but I need to know. Dad, I *need* to know."

Mr. Jarvis had to tell his daughter the truth. Gently he said, "Honey, your baby cousin passed away a half-hour ago."

The new few hours were the most painful of Jayme's life. The entire team gathered around and said a prayer for her. One of the coaches then drove her home. Meanwhile, the Red Team had no choice but to play the game. In a tribute to Alida, they put up *sixteen* runs. They crushed their opponents by a score of 16-3. They were in the championship game, which was set for the next day.

The Championship Game

Jayme woke up early the next morning. She wanted to believe that it had all been a bad dream. Her pillow, though, was wet with tears. Jayme realized that her life would never be the same.

A few minutes later, Jayme's mother entered the room with some food. Mrs. Jarvis put the tray down and sat by the edge of the bed. She and Jayme talked for a long time. Jayme said, "Mom, today is the championship game. I shouldn't play, should I?"

"Honey, that's a decision only you can make," Mrs Jarvis replied. "But ask yourself one question: What would Alida want you to do?"

Inspired by her mother's words, Jayme immediately started to get up out of bed. "That's easy, Mom," she said. "Alida would want me to play for her today. She would want the whole family together, watching."

An hour later, Jayme stepped out of the car in her uniform. Three other cars of family members were right behind her. They had all come to the ballpark to pay tribute to Alida. When Jayme's teammates saw her, they ran over and hugged her. They had made a huge card, expressing their sympathies to Jayme and her family. When Jayme saw it, she smiled through her tears.

Later, when Jayme stepped up to the plate, she was very emotional. The pitcher delivered a blazing pitch for strike one. After a couple of balls, she threw another heater, which Jayme fouled off. The count was now 2 and 2.

Usually, with two strikes on her, Jayme shortens her swing a little. She tries to punch it into play. However, something deep inside of her was building up. When the pitcher threw another fastball, Jayme swung as hard as she could. The explosion of the bat striking the ball was loud. Everyone knew instantly that it was a home run.

As Jayme rounded the bases, tears streamed down her face. She looked up to the sky. The people in the stands knew what had just happened. Jayme had sent a ball into the heavens. It was a gift for her beautiful cousin. The crowd erupted into the loudest cheering that had been heard all season long.

When Jayme's feet touched home plate, the entire team was waiting to greet her. They hugged her and yelled, "You did it for Alida!" Jayme felt like Alida was looking down on her. The Red Team went on to win the championship and qualify for the nationals. Jayme was awarded the MVP of the tournament. She held the trophy close to her heart and whispered, "This is for you, Alida."

A Fitting Tribute

Jayme Jarvis has experienced the best of times and the worst of times. But through it all, she has stayed strong. Jayme didn't let the tragedy in her life destroy her. That's a fitting tribute to Alida.

Jayme and the Red Team ended up placing second in the national tournament. It was just two months after the funeral. "I owe it to Alida to accomplish great things in my life," Jayme says. "It's like I'm doing it for *both* of us now. I'm not going to let her down."

As she points toward a bright future, Jayme has big plans. She hopes to get a scholarship to either UCLA or the University of Arizona. With her high grade point average and her softball skills, she has an excellent chance. Jayme, now fifteen years old, has also thought about what she wants to do after college: "I've been thinking of going into sports medicine, or maybe even psychology."

Although she is focused on her future, Jayme never forgets the past. Not a day goes by that she doesn't think about Alida. Sometimes she laughs, and other times she cries. But she always keeps Alida close to her heart.

Jayme is a great student and an outstanding softball player. Alida would be proud that her older cousin is a worthy role model . . . and a future star of America.

Heart of a Giant

Land of the Midnight Sun

Sixteen-year-old Jack Pearce and his father stepped outside of their house. They shielded their eyes from the warm Alaskan sun. As they started to work on Jack's truck, they talked about hockey. Like Jack, Mr. Pearce is a huge hockey fan. He's also a hockey coach. As a matter of fact, he's been Jack's coach for almost ten years.

They continued to work on the truck. There's always plenty to do. They tinker with the engine and fine-tune the brakes. They've even been talking about giving it a new paint job. Like hockey, working on the truck is something Jack and his dad do for fun. It also gives them the chance to spend time together.

A little while later, two of Jack's best friends showed up at the house. "Dad, Jeremy and Michael are gonna crash here tonight. Is that cool with you?" Jack asked, bumping knuckles with his two buddies.

"Sure," Mr. Pearce laughed. "Just don't keep your mom and me up all night!"

The guys grabbed a basketball from the corner of the garage. They started to shoot around. They ended up playing a game of twenty-one. Of course, they bumped into each other a lot. That's what happens when hockey players play basketball—body-checking somehow becomes part of the game!

Jack Pearce of Eagle River, Alaska, is shown in a familiar pose—celebrating after scoring a goal!

*Photo courtesy of John Hitchcock.

It was beautiful outside. Sunshine poured down on them from the bright blue sky. A bald eagle flew overhead. People who live in Alaska are used to this. Still, Jack and his friends stopped for a moment to appreciate the sight. Later, they went inside to grab some sodas and listen to music. Sunlight was still streaming in through the living room windows. This wasn't unusual . . . except that it was close to midnight!

In Alaska, it can stay light during the summer for close to twenty hours a day. It can also get very cold there during the winter. Some kids think of Alaska only as a snowy state that is home to polar bears. However, there is so much more to Alaska. "It's not like people picture it at all," Jack says with a smile. "Our lives are the same as people in other states." He's right. There are malls, fast-food restaurants, video stores, and everything else people are used to.

Alaska's location is unique. It's close to the North Pole. That's what causes the sun to stay out so long during the summer months. Visitors have been coming to Alaska for many years. One reason is the natural beauty that can be found there. Alaska offers a clear, untouched view of nature. People never run out of things to do. Some favorite activities are camping, hiking, and watching the wildlife.

For Jack, Alaska is definitely home. "What an awesome place to grow up," he says. "There's just so much to do here." It's really true, and Jack has a ton of cool hobbies. Sure, he enjoys working on his truck or hanging out with his friends. But that's not all. He's usually at school or at the ice rink playing the game he loves . . . hockey.

Captain Jack

The two captains were called to center ice before the championship game started. Jack Pearce skated out to represent the Eagle River Glacier Bears. For the second year in a row, he had been voted captain by his teammates. Jack takes this honor seriously. He tries to be a leader both on and off the ice.

At center ice, Doug Lassiter shook Jack's hand. Doug was the captain of the Mighty Moose. They were the best team in the league. Players on their team were seventeen and eighteen years old. The Glacier Bears were younger. Their players were fifteen and sixteen years old. That gave Doug and his teammates an edge.

Everyone in the crowd knew that the Glacier Bears were facing a tough challenge. True, they were a talented team. Still, they had to try to overcome the strength and power of the Mighty Moose. That wasn't going to be easy. Jack had a further disadvantage, being only five feet seven. Doug was an eighteen-year-old high school senior. He had been shaving for several years. At six feet four, he towered over Jack. He outweighed him by at least thirty pounds.

A few minutes later, Jack skated back out to

center ice with the Glacier Bears. It was time for the beginning of the game. Jack turned to face his teammates. "Let's go, guys," he exclaimed with emotion. "It's the championship game! I don't care if I get a bloody nose, or lose a couple of teeth. All I know is that I'm gonna fight hard. As far as I'm concerned, that's what hockey is all about. Who's with me?"

Inspired, the Glacier Bears began to chant and slap high-fives. Jeremy bumped Jack in the chest and said, "We're with you, Captain Jack. Let's give these guys all we've got." Ten seconds later, the puck was dropped and the game was under way.

Hobbies

Jack Pearce has a wide variety of hobbies. In the summer, he goes hiking, biking, camping, and rollerblading. In the winter, there's not as much free time because of hockey and school. Jack's schedule is busy. When he gets the chance, though, he loves many different things. Sometimes he goes snowboarding, or cruises around on a snowmobile.

Another of Jack's favorite activities is hunting with his father. Hunting is a sport that requires responsibility and care. "My dad and I took the Alaska hunter safety course. We know what we're supposed to do and not do," Jack says. "Like all Alaskans, we're proud of our environment and we try to protect it."

When he's not playing hockey, Jack also enjoys fishing. His home is close to the beautiful Kenai

River. He and his friends fish there every chance they get. "Fishing is a big thing in Alaska and I've always loved it," Jack explains. "We catch salmon and trout and even halibut. It's cool to bring my catch home and ask my mom to cook it up. It's the most delicious thing in the world."

Fishing, a peaceful activity, is a nice balance in Jack's life. "Hockey is so rough, so physical," he says. "For me, fishing is relaxing. To be out in the wilderness and enjoying nature—what can be better? My friends and I chill out there. We don't worry about what time it is or what problems we may have. When I get back home, my mind is clear and refreshed. Then I'm ready to get back out there on the ice."

Heart of a Giant

The Glacier Bears did not defeat the Mighty Moose in the championship game that day. After all, the Mighty Moose were older, bigger, and stronger than the Glacier Bears. Still, that didn't stop Jack and his teammates from giving 100 percent. But when it was over, the top-ranked Mighty Moose were the ones to walk away with the trophy.

The Glacier Bears ended up with the second-place trophy. However, they had a reason to celebrate after the game. The team had played hard and shown the heart of a giant. From the moment the puck was dropped, Jack played with intensity. He wanted to show everybody that this was going to be a competitive game. Jack's determination was rewarded. Just three minutes into the game, an opportunity developed.

It happened when a Mighty Moose defenseman lost the puck at mid-ice. Jack swooped in and gained control of it. He tore down the ice with only Doug Lassiter to beat. With the crowd screaming, he shook free from Doug with some fancy stick work. Winding up, Jack hit the hardest slap shot of his life. The goalie tried to stab the puck from mid-air, but it was moving too fast. The red light went on and the crowd erupted. 1-0, Glacier Bears!

The Mighty Moose came right back, scoring to tie the game. But the Glacier Bears, inspired by Jack's intensity, started to play even harder. The Mighty Moose coaching staff looked shocked. People in the crowd were amazed as well. They cheered for the underdog Glacier Bears. Jack's team fell behind, but they kept fighting back. It was a struggle because the Mighty Moose were so talented.

The Glacier Bears scored a late goal to take the game to overtime. The Mighty Moose finally pulled it out, though. Still, the Glacier Bears felt as if *they* were the winners. The crowd gave them a loud round of applause after the game. So did the entire Mighty Moose team.

Nobody was prouder that night than Jack Pearce. He hadn't been intimidated by Doug Lassiter and the huge Mighty Moose. Jack learned that you don't win every time. You don't always come out on top. But it's important to be the best athlete and person you can possibly be.

Setting Big Goals

Jack spends many days knee-deep in the Kenai River, just kicking back and fishing. Sometimes, he looks upward to the blue Alaskan sky. At these moments, he feels very inspired. "I think about all kinds of different things," Jack explains. "I try and imagine where life is going to take me."

There's no doubt that Jack's journey will lead him to some amazing places. An honor student, he is interested in architecture. Many years from now, after earning a college degree, he'll be on his way. He pictures himself in the future designing buildings. That would truly be a rewarding and exciting career.

Architecture, of course, is a complicated field. It requires a great deal of training and education. That's why Jack is already thinking about college. He has set a big goal for himself. He wants to go to the University of Alaska at Anchorage. It's a fine local college. Also, the top 10 percent of high school seniors in Alaska receive scholarships. Naturally, Jack wants to qualify.

"I'm in the running," he says, looking up from a huge stack of schoolbooks. "Right now I'm just outside of the top ten. So I've got to hit the books just a little bit harder. I'm confident I can make it."

Jack is definitely going to make it. He's going

Gone fishing!

to do many awesome things in the future. Hockey has taught him a lot. He's learned to play hard at all times—even when he's one of the smaller kids on the ice. Jack knows that there are kids all across the country that struggle with things. Some of them are too tall, or too short, or not good enough at something. He doesn't think that should stop them. "My advice is to set a goal and then go for it," he says.

These are deep words from a teenager who practices what he preaches. He's always setting big goals for himself—like trying to earn a scholarship. Or dreaming about creating newer and better buildings. Jack even tries to catch the biggest fish out in the river! No matter what, he continues to chase down his dreams. Jack Pearce is a kid with the heart of a giant. That makes him a giant success—and a future star of America!

Jordie Karlinski, above, and her brother
Teddy Karlinski, below, are two of the
top young snowboarders in America.

Getting Air Up There

Photo Finish

Jordan Karlinski was nervous. She was standing at the top of the mountain inside the starting gate. She was wearing a heavy jacket and gloves. The freezing cold had fogged up her goggles. Her heart was thumping.

Jordan—or Jordie, as everyone calls her—wasn't alone at the top of the mountain. She was standing next to some of the best snowboarders in the United States. Some of them were her friends, but that didn't matter right now. This was about competition, not friendship.

Snowboarding fans had lined the slope. There was excitement and anticipation in the air. This event was called boardercross. It was a race on a course that was filled with turns and jumps. The competitors would be speeding down the mountain.

Fifteen-year-old Jordan Karlinski and the other women were competing for an awesome prize. The winner would get to compete at the winter X-Games. They were going to be held on Buttermilk Mountain in Aspen, Colorado. That's a beautiful location. It's also near Jordie's house. She happens to live just a few miles away from that mountain.

Jordie had been dreaming about the X-Games for a long time. This was her chance, but she realized that winning wasn't going to be easy. She was the youngest competitor in the field. A couple of the other girls were famous in the snowboarding world. Jordie focused on the finish line. She *had* to get there first. She wanted it more than anything else she had ever wanted.

It was helpful that Teddy was there cheering her on. He's her older brother, and a champion snowboarder as well. He had given Jordie a pep talk before the race. Then he went and joined some of the other spectators near the bottom of the run. It was time for Jordie to show what she could do.

Suddenly the starting gate dropped. The competitors shot out of the gate like bolts of lightening. The wind was fierce and extremely loud. Jordie couldn't even hear the huge crowd cheering. She tore down the mountain.

Although Jordie was slightly in the lead, Sarah was coming on strong. She passed Jordie at the midway point. Soon they were coming up on the last turn. Jordie pumped faster and increased her speed. She ignored how tired her arms and legs felt. Suddenly she was neck and neck with Sarah. They were in the final stretch. Jordie forced herself to reach out and inch her way past Sarah. Over on the sideline, Teddy yelled, "Keep going, Jordie, you're almost there!"

A moment later, Jordie and Sarah crossed the finish line in a photo finish. Everyone looked to the judges. The next couple of minutes were tense. Then the judges put the name "Jordan Karlinski" up on the big scoreboard. The crowd went crazy. Jordie looked over at Teddy and happily gave him the thumbs-up sign. He pumped his fist and shouted with joy. Jordie was headed to the X-Games.

Aspen, Colorado

It was a little shocking at first. Seven-year-old Teddy and six-year-old Jordie found out that they were moving. They were upset, of course. They were used to living in beautiful, sunny California. They had fun playing outside with their friends, even in the middle of winter. Now they were moving to—where? To the mountains, up in Aspen, Colorado?

Jordie tried to imagine what her new life would be like. As for Teddy, he wondered if the kids at his new school would be cool. Their parents encouraged them. They explained that there would even be more opportunities to go skiing. This was something both children enjoyed. Teddy and Jordie had actually been skiing for most of their lives. Along with their oldest sister, Alex, they showed a real talent on the snow.

The family finally settled in their new house in Aspen. Teddy and Jordie started adjusting to living in cold and snowy weather. They quickly became friends with the kids in their neighborhood. Sure, at times they missed certain things about California … like being able to run outside without putting on a heavy jacket.

Still, what kids don't love playing in the snow, or sledding with their friends?

One of the main activities in Aspen is skiing. Because of their skiing experience, Teddy and Jordie fit right in. They hit the slopes whenever they had a chance. They also found time for other hobbies. Teddy took up golf, a sport he still plays. It just so happens that he's *really* good. Some people think he could wind up as a pro golfer. When Jordie is not out on the snow, she also enjoys other things. She plays soccer and Ultimate Frisbee, and hangs out with her friends.

Everything changed for Teddy and Jordie when their parents introduced them to snowboarding. It's a sport that combines surfing, skiing, and skateboarding. Snowboarders use a board that looks like a cross between a skateboard and a surfboard. They ride on the snow the way a skateboarder rips it on the pavement. Although snowboarding is difficult to learn, it's a total rush.

Teddy and Jordie soon discovered just *how* big of a rush it was. When they did, their lives were changed forever. They had discovered their true passion.

Big Air

"Dude, Teddy, aren't you nervous? I mean, Matt Peterson and a bunch of excellent riders are here. And you're the youngest guy in the field." Teddy's best friend, Kyle Duffy, was looking at the slope.

"Yeah, I'm a little nervous," Teddy admitted. "But look, Kyle, I definitely have an advantage. The contest is right here in Aspen. I had a chance to check out the jump a couple of days ago. I've been visualizing it in my mind. I can *see* myself in the air and what tricks I'm going to do."

It was certainly an advantage that the contest was in Teddy's hometown. Still, it wasn't going to be easy. The event, known as Big Air, was a sixty-five-foot jump off a platform. The snowboarders would start at the top of the mountain. They would build up speed, and then fly off the platform. The goal was to land smoothly on the snow below. While in midair, each competitor would break out his most impressive tricks.

After the first two rounds, four people scored high enough to advance to the semi-finals. Teddy was one of them. On his next jump, he landed a 720 with a heel grab. The crowd cheered and Teddy smiled with satisfaction. After the other three boarders had their chance, the judges announced the results. Teddy Karlinski was in the finals. His opponent was none other than the famous Matt Peterson!

Teddy knew that he was an underdog. He watched as Matt skillfully landed an insane 720 nose grab with a poke. That earned a 9.8 from the judges—almost a perfect score. Teddy was stunned. He looked over to his best friend, Kyle, whose mouth was wide open. Then Teddy glanced at Jordie, who nodded her head. "Forget about Matt's jump and concentrate on what you've been practicing," she said. "You can do it. Just go big. *Real* big."

Teddy was determined as he looked down the hill at the huge sixty-five-foot jump. In his mind he repeated his sister's words: *Go big.* He was ready. Suddenly, Teddy was racing down the mountain. He gathered a lot of speed. As he flew through the air, Teddy did *three* full rotations off-axis. Boom! His board gracefully crashed down onto the snow—he landed it perfectly.

Everybody went crazy with applause. Jordie was shouting with joy, and Teddy's parents were grinning from ear to ear. It didn't take the judges long. They held up their cards, which showed that they had given Teddy a perfect 10. He had won the contest by doing the near-impossible. Of course, to Teddy and Jordie Karlinski, *nothing* is impossible. Especially when they're up in the snowy mountains, getting air up there.

Lessons Learned

Life has been very good to Teddy and Jordie Karlinski. They have a great family, and they are tremendous athletes. They've also had the opportunity to do a lot of really cool things. A year ago, for example, they received a prestigious honor. The USA Snowboard Association selected them to the All-American Team. It was headed to the Junior World Championships . . . in Italy. It was one of the most exciting experiences of their entire lives. Teddy and Jordie brought home medals in every event they entered. They helped their team win the competition.

Obviously it's a lot of fun to live in a mountain paradise like Aspen. Still, there are many challenges to deal with. Teddy and Jordan have had their share of disappointments and even heartbreak. They've responded with the same courage they demonstrate on the snow.

Jordie, now sixteen years old, has been on several teams as the only girl. Making things even more difficult, she is often the youngest team member. It's a compliment to her skill that teams keep asking her to join. Of course it's always nice when Teddy is there to stick up for her. But there have been times that Jordie had to take care of herself. "It can be a little intimidating," she says, "but I just keep at it."

More important was a serious incident that occurred a couple of years ago. It shook Teddy and Jordie up more than anything that had ever happened to them. One of Teddy's best friends was killed in a car accident. The heartbreak was felt by everyone in Aspen. Seventeen-year-old Teddy still has a heavy heart when he thinks about his friend David Miller. It's been difficult to move on with his life, but he's had no choice. However, Teddy feels that a critical message must be passed along to kids.

"The accident happened when David's friend tried to pass another car. He should have stayed in his own lane. He should have just traveled the speed limit," Teddy says in a low voice. "David wasn't wearing a seatbelt. The driver lost control of the car and it flipped over. David was thrown from the car."

Teddy forces himself to finish the story. He wants to explain the lesson that goes along with it. "It's very, very simple: a car is not a toy. It's not something to mess around with. Kids have to remember that. They also need to wear their seatbelt all the time. If they do that, they'll be okay. Don't think it can't happen to you, or to someone you care about. I really hope kids are smart about that kind of stuff." Jordie nods in agreement.

Teddy and Jordie hanging out after a long day of snowboarding on Mt. Hood in Oregon.

It's nice to see Teddy and Jordie deliver such a powerful and worthwhile message. They carry their inspiring outlook on life with them wherever they go. Their hearts will always belong to the snow-capped mountains they love so dearly. Their hopes and dreams will always be getting air up there. That's why Teddy and Jordan Karlinski are future stars of America.

**Ryan Russo-Brayman, of Florida,
prepares to do his XMA form.**

* Photo courtesy of Michael Grimes Photography.

Taking it to the Extreme

XMA

It was a sunny day in Orlando, Florida. That's the home of Disney World, Universal Studios, and other fun attractions. The parade route on Main Street was lined with happy kids and their parents. There were jugglers, clowns, acrobats, and musicians. Yet there was one person who ended up drawing most of the attention. His name was Ryan Russo-Brayman.

Fourteen-year-old Ryan was in the parade representing Brayman's Martial Arts. That's a school owned by his parents. Ryan stood proudly in his bright silver and black uniform. He attracted a lot of attention . . . especially when he started performing his amazing XMA routine.

XMA stands for Extreme Martial Arts. It's a blend of martial arts, self-defense, gymnastics, and dance. It hasn't been around for a long time, but it's starting to become popular. Ryan is trained in many forms of martial arts, but XMA is his favorite.

Ryan is a totally modest and respectful kid. He turns into a bundle of energy, though, whenever he's performing. Today was no different. He drew gasps of wonder and appreciation from the crowd. He used a bow staff, which is a long pole made of hard wood. Waving it skillfully, he bounced around to a song called "Kung Fu Fighting." He twirled the bow staff high in

51

the air.

XMA is all about movement and perfect timing. It's based on self-defense, which is a big part of martial arts. When Ryan does a flip or a cartwheel, he has to land perfectly. This is important in self-defense. A martial artist always has to be in good position. That way he can use other moves to hold off an attacker.

Ryan was moving to the music and handling the bow staff with care. It was a real treat for the fans. This was *far* more interesting than anything else that was going on. A boy named Mike tugged at his mother's sleeve and whispered loudly, "Mom, that looks so cool! Can I take martial arts?" Ryan grinned. He's used to reactions like that. After all, martial arts *are* cool. They've changed Ryan's life . . . and he's committed to helping others do the very same thing.

Student and Teacher

"A student of martial arts should also be a *teacher*," Ryan explains. He makes his point by telling a story about Francis Marshall. Francis is an eleven-year-old who has been studying martial arts for a couple of years. Ryan is one of Francis' teachers.

One day Francis and his mother showed up at Brayman's Martial Arts. Mrs. Marshall was searching for a way to help her son. Francis, a curly-haired kid with thick glasses, was shy and overweight. He was getting picked on at school almost every day. The teasing was bad enough, but things got even worse.

Getting beat up by two boys on the playground was the final straw.

Master Instructor Ken Brayman, Ryan's father, took a long look at Francis. He realized that Francis was clumsy and out of shape. Mr. Brayman saw an opportunity. He asked Ryan to tell Francis a little bit about martial arts. Ryan smiled and began talking. He explained that there's a place for everyone in martial arts. "All you have to do is give your best effort," Ryan told Francis. "Martial arts will help you achieve things you would have thought were impossible."

Francis asked if Ryan used his training to beat up other kids. Ryan laughed. "No," he answered. "Martial arts is the opposite of violence. It's about having the confidence to walk away from trouble. I would use my skills only if I had to protect myself." Looking at Francis, Ryan added, "Martial arts has helped me to become more focused. It's made me happier, healthier, and stronger. Trust me, dude, it will do the same for you."

Mr. Brayman was very pleased. He couldn't have said it better himself. He's proud that Ryan has come such a long way. It's cool that Ryan is now having a big impact on other kids.

It wasn't easy at first, because Francis *was* out of shape. But slowly, as Ryan had predicted, things began to turn around. With Ryan's encouragement, Francis started losing weight, eating better, and training harder. Within a year, he was a brand new kid. The bullies at school didn't come near him anymore. Francis had become popular at school for the first time in his life.

Francis refuses to take credit for the amazing change in his life. "I owe it all to Ryan," he says without hesitation. "He's the coolest kid I've ever known. He inspires me to work hard and be a better person. Ryan is the best!"

Black Belt Spectacular

Ryan and his friend, seventeen-year-old Jeremy, were backstage warming up. They were waiting for the Black Belt Spectacular to begin. Ryan's dad, Mr. Brayman—Mr. B, as everyone calls him—came backstage. He walked up to Ryan and Jeremy with a big smile on his face. His students were getting their *full adult* black belts. For Ryan, this was happening at the age of fourteen! This was definitely a special evening.

Mr. B then walked onto the stage. The rest of Ryan's family was in the audience, cameras in hand. "Welcome, friends," Mr. B began. "We're here to honor the achievement of black belt by Mr. Ryan and Mr. Jeremy. They passed every physical test. They've also pledged to live by the principles of a black belt."

As Ryan and Jeremy stepped forward, the audience erupted with applause. Ryan glanced at his father, and then at his mother out in the audience. This was an awesome moment that they would remember for the rest of their lives. Mr. B continued, "Mr. Ryan and Mr. Jeremy, we're all very proud of you. Now I ask you to perform your black belt routines for us."

The next hour was a stunning display of skill. After Ryan and Jeremy bowed to each other, they began their performance. It featured everything they had learned for their tests. They started out by showing how to take weapons away from sudden attackers.

Each movement had been planned to avoid injury. First, an opponent swung a knife in Ryan's direction. Ryan quickly moved to his left, avoiding the knife. The attacker tried again, but Ryan saw it coming. He grabbed his opponent's wrist. Then he used his other hand to snatch the knife away. He then bowed to his opponent—a sign of respect.

Next, Ryan and Jeremy did their exciting XMA routine. Then it was time for the big finish, called the "breakthrough." Ryan used the courage and confidence he had learned from the eight-week black belt test. He broke a one-inch slab of concrete with his bare hand!

Finally, there was a very emotional moment. Mr. B presented his son with a black belt, and a black belt sword. Ryan had truly earned his black belt. He had done it the same way he's earned everything else—through hard work.

Overcoming Obstacles

When Ryan arrived at the auditorium, he looked

at the board. He groaned when he saw Cathy Green's name on it. Cathy is one of the leading martial artists for their age group. She had defeated Ryan many times before in this type of competition. It wasn't hand-to-hand combat. Instead, it focused on martial arts form and technique. Would she once again stand in the winner's circle, at Ryan's expense?

The scene was the prestigious Kicks USA Regionals tournament. Although Ryan was a little intimidated at first, he quickly became energized. An opportunity lay before him. "Martial arts is all about overcoming obstacles," he says. "I realized that I was ready to face the challenge of squaring off against Cathy. I *really* wanted to win."

Things moved steadily toward a showdown between the two champions. It was a little nerve-wracking because they had been placed on the largest stage. This meant that they were the main attraction. Everyone was watching. Ryan tried to keep his focus on form and technique.

The contest featured Ryan's specialty: weapons. "There's something very special about the weapons competition," he explains. "They are so difficult because they're an extension of your body. If you don't move the right way, you'll hit yourself . . . hard!"

Today Ryan was once again using his trusty bow staff. He handled it with skill. People were amazed at his accurate form. The whooshing sound of the bow staff cut through the air. By the time Ryan was announced as one of the finalists, a huge crowd was watching. Ryan didn't even have to ask his dad who his opponent was going to be. He just knew. It was Cathy Green.

Like Ryan, Cathy handled her weapon with skill. When she did her form, the crowd cheered loudly. The three judges held up their cards. She had been given the remarkable score of 8, 8, and 9. Cathy joyfully pumped her fist. After all, 9 is the highest score you can get. To win, Ryan would have to pull off a near-miracle.

Taking a deep breath, Ryan went to work. Although there were people yelling and shouting for him, he didn't even hear them. He was too busy concentrating. It felt like only he and his bow staff existed. The result was pure magic. "I did my form, and when I was finished I felt great," he says. "Still, I had no idea if I would win. I couldn't even remember what I had done. That's how focused I was."

Everyone was amazed. Ryan Russo-Brayman had performed weapons technique and form with tremendous skill. The judges held up their scorecards. The people in the audience jumped to their feet, giving Ryan a standing ovation. He had received a rare *perfect* score: 9, 9, and 9.

Ryan shouted with joy when he saw his score. "I was so excited!" he remembers. "I realized that all my hard work and discipline had led to my success. It all paid off for me that day. I don't think I'll ever forget it." Neither will anyone else who saw his unbelievable performance.

The True Spirit of Martial Arts

Ryan Russo-Brayman first became interested in martial arts a long time ago. Yet he never could have dreamed where it would lead him. The best part is the good feeling he gets by helping other people. That's the *true* spirit of martial arts. It's also why everyone looks to Ryan as a role model. Because of martial arts, he makes a difference in the lives of kids like Francis.

Ryan is as quick with a smile as he is with one of his XMA moves. The future looks incredibly bright for him. There's a chance that XMA will be included in the X-Games in the near future. If so, Ryan will definitely be trying out. He's setting his sights even higher, though. Could XMA ever become an Olympic sport? "That would be totally awesome," Ryan says with a wide grin.

For now, Ryan continues to work hard and enjoy life. When he's not practicing martial arts, he has plenty of hobbies. He likes skateboarding, video games, and hanging out with his friends. In the future, he'll have many excellent opportunities. He plans to go to college and he's even thinking about becoming a lawyer.

Ryan will probably never stray too far away from martial arts. At his black belt ceremony, he told the crowd what he had learned. "The principles of the black belt are to never give up. To respect the ability of others and be willing to help guide them. To be a person that others can always rely on. To be proud of your accomplishments. To always try to do your best."

Ryan Russo-Brayman's entire life is an example of these values. He's taking it to the extreme with martial arts. It gives him a powerful sense of pride and purpose. He has talent, and an interest in helping out. That makes him a star . . . a future star of America!

Ryan shows his athleticism during an XMA demonstration.

*Photo courtesy of Michael Grimes Photography.

Lacey Baker of California,
loves to get air. She does insane tricks
at the skate park or right on the street!

Street Skater

The Skate Park

Lacey Baker rushed home from school and ran straight to her room. She put her schoolbooks on her desk. Grabbing her skateboard and helmet, she kissed her mom good-bye. Lacey bolted out the front door just as her friend Evan drove up with his mom. "Perfect timing," Lacey said. "Let's roll."

There's nothing quite like a Friday afternoon. School is over, which means no homework and an entire weekend to have fun. Lacey lives in California, where it's almost always sunny and beautiful outside. These are perfect conditions for a street skater. And thirteen-year-old Lacey Baker is *definitely* a street skater.

Evan's mom dropped them off at the skateboard park. It's an excellent place to skate. The concrete is very smooth, and there are rails and stairs. When Lacey and Evan arrived, they were greeted by a bunch of their friends. Lacey was amped. Wasting no time, she got out there and started skating.

Lacey is one of the top skateboarders in California for her age. She skates because it's what she loves to do. "I just want to have fun," Lacey explains. "When I see somebody do an insane trick, I want to learn it too. I'll start by trying it on the ground—on flat land. When I start to get the hang of it, I'll take it to a higher level. For example, I might try to take off on the stairs. It's such a great feeling when I finally get it."

Lacey can remember the first time she landed a trick. It was only a kick flip, but that's pretty good for a beginner. She was just ten years old. "I'll never forget it," Lacey says with a smile. "It was a Saturday, a very cloudy day. I was skating on the street and all of a sudden, boom! I landed my first kick flip. It was awesome. I knew right then that skateboarding was for me."

Lacey has come a long way from landing simple kick flips. These days she's setting her sights higher. She's learning a switch-stance front-side 180 kick-flip. Lacey also wants to master a front-side crooked grind. That's what she was working on at the skateboard park with her friend Evan. She kept trying, over and over again, until she finally got it. Although Lacey doesn't try to attract attention, people were staring at her in awe. Skateboarding fans know that this street skater is going all the way to the top.

An Athletic Girl

Thirteen-year-old Lacey Baker has been skating for more than half her life. An athletic girl, she got her first skateboard at age five. She has always loved being outdoors. Lacey's mother remembers that Lacey was rollerblading at age four. She had absolutely no fear. Ms. Baker proves this point by recalling something interesting that happened a long time ago.

Ms. Baker had taken her kids on a family vacation. They were camping near the Colorado River. It was summer and the weather was beautiful. Someone there had a ski skimmer. That's a special ski for a beginner at water-skiing. Many of the children that gathered around the boat were intimidated. Most of them were too scared to try it. But not six-year-old Lacey. "She insisted on trying," Ms. Baker laughs. "Lacey ended up having the longest run of any water-skier there!"

This was a sign of things to come. In the years that followed, Lacey was always outside. She was into skating, climbing huge trees, and playing basketball with the older boys. And when Ryan Miller came into her life, things *really* started to take off. Twenty-six-year-old Ryan is Lacey's coach. He's also a friend and fellow skateboarder. He spends time with Lacey working on her form and technique.

Lacey and Ryan met four years ago. Ms. Baker took Lacey to a skateboarding class. Ryan was the teacher. As soon as he saw Lacey skate, Ryan took her mother aside. "I have to be honest with you, Ms. Baker," Ryan remembers saying. "Lacey is *much* too good for this class. She's welcome to stay, but I think it will probably be boring for her."

Lacey was having a good time, so she decided to stay. Ryan ended up becoming friends with her whole family. At the time, Lacey was getting ready to start entering contests. She didn't have a coach, but she definitely needed one. Her mother talked to Ryan about it. The next thing Lacey knew, she had a high-quality coach. Ryan teaches her new tricks and prepares her for competition.

Lacey owes her success to hard work, and also to the great people around her. Besides her family, Ryan is at the top of the list. She says, "Ryan Miller is the best person in the world! If it weren't for him, I wouldn't be where I am today." Considering how far she's come, that's quite a compliment.

The Commercial

Like all kids, Lacey enjoys watching television. She even likes the commercials . . . especially the one she's in! Lacey's skill as a skateboarder has given her the opportunity to do some cool things. Being on television is one of those things.

It all started pretty simply. Lacey heard that her friend Gwen was auditioning for a commercial. Lacey called to wish her luck. Soon after that, Gwen's mom called Lacey's mom with some exciting news. Gwen had received a "callback." That meant the producers were interested and wanted Gwen to do a second audition.

There was one other thing. The commercial needed an awesome girl skateboarder. Gwen's mom told Lacey's mom, "Lacey is the best skateboarder around. You *have* to get her out to the skate park."

The next day, Lacey showed up with her mom. When it was her turn to skate, she landed some amazing tricks. The producers were blown away. One of them talked to Lacey's mom and took down her phone number.

Lacey was getting a taste of what an actor goes through after an audition. They wait around, hoping that the phone will ring with good news. Even famous actors have been turned down many times in their lives. Lacey was certain that she wasn't going to get the commercial. "A couple of days went by and we didn't hear anything. I figured they had chosen someone else. I was bummed. I had gotten pretty psyched about the chance to be in a real commercial."

But her chance *did* come. The next day, the producer called. When Ms. Baker put down the phone, Lacey could barely speak. "Did I get it?" she asked in a whisper. Her mom didn't even respond—she just smiled. Lacey was so happy that she jumped out of her chair. "Oh my gosh, I can't believe it. I'm going to be on television!"

When the day of the filming arrived, Lacey was nervous. "At first I didn't know if I was going to be able to do it. But the director told me to relax. He said to pretend that this was like any other normal day. So I just started skating. Pretty soon I forgot all about the cameras. They filmed me landing a hard flip, and dropping in on a six-foot quarter pipe. It ended up being a very cool day."

It was even more exciting a couple of months later. Lacey and her family saw her on television for the first time. Naturally, the phone started ringing. People were asking, "Hey, Lacey, was that *you* I just saw on television?" Overall, the experience was fun and rewarding. So has a television star been born? "Nah," Lacey says with a big grin, "I'm a skater. Nothing's ever gonna change that."

The Gallaz Skate Jam

Lacey arrived with her mom at the Gallaz Skate Jam in Torrance, California. She wasn't expecting much. For one thing, it was cold and rainy. That makes it more difficult to land awesome tricks. Also, this competition had attracted many outstanding skaters. They were all trying to win the first prize—a trip to Australia.

Early on, it seemed like this wasn't Lacey's day. She started with a warm-up run, but wasn't able to land anything good. "I didn't have a great run," she admits. "I had fallen pretty far behind. Luckily, the jam session turned everything around for me." This was the most important part of the competition. In the jam session, all rules were tossed out the window. Instead, the skateboarders could do whatever tricks or flips they wanted. As a street skater, this was definitely Lacey's best event.

Suddenly Lacey was feeling confident and loose. She began to make a huge comeback. The fans started cheering and rooting for her. Finally, with time running out, Lacey went for it all. She landed an insane front-side flip off a three-and-a-half foot drop. The fans went crazy! At that moment, everybody knew that the contest was over. Nobody was going to top Lacey. With her inspiring comeback, she had earned the trip to Australia.

The awards presentation was amazing. They called Lacey's name and she went up in front of the large crowd. She was speechless at first. Lacey was delighted to share this moment with the special people in her life. This includes her mom and Ryan, of course.

For her first place finish at the Gallaz Skate Jam, Lacey won a round trip ticket to Australia!

In the car on the way home, Lacey and her mom celebrated. Ms. Baker said, "The *real* prize was hearing your name called out as the winner. Everything else—even the trip to Australia—is just icing on the cake. The thing you're going to remember is the feeling of accomplishment. It shows that you can be a success in life." Lacey smiled and nodded her head. Her mom was right. Working hard to reach a goal *is* a pretty cool feeling.

Life Rushes On

It's true that much of Lacey's time is spent landing flips, grinds, and jumps. But there's a lot more to her than skateboarding. For one thing, she takes school very seriously. One of her mom's rules is that you come home and do your homework. *Then* you go out and skate. When Lacey went on her trip to Australia, she had to miss two weeks of school. Problem? No way. Lacey took her schoolbooks along!

Lacey also has many hobbies. An excellent artist, she draws pictures of skateboarders. Lacey and her friends also enjoy hackey sack. It's a game that uses a small ball. Players try to keep it in the air without using their hands.

Lacey is looking forward to an exciting future. She graduated from the eighth grade last spring with a grade point average of 3.2. She has everything all planned out. "Obviously my dream is to become a pro skater," she explains. "After my career in skateboarding is over, I'll become a teacher. I'm really interested in working with kids."

So life rushes on for street skater Lacey Baker. "I'm grateful for everything I have," she says. "I'm always trying to improve and make myself a better person. No matter what happens, I just keep going. That's my message for kids . . . *never* quit."

That's a powerful message. That's why Lacey is a popular kid, a promising athlete . . . and a future star of America!

Nuno Muandumba of Arizona, is an
amazing scorer. Showing his tremendous
athletic ability, "Mr. Smooth" glides to
the rim for easy baskets.

Mr. Smooth

Intense Competitor

The gym was packed with fans of the Arizona Blaze. People were stamping their feet and cheering before the game even started. Although it was great to have so much support, it also put extra pressure on the team. This was the championship game of the tournament. It didn't seem likely that the Blaze could pull off an upset against the Flyers. After all, the Flyers hadn't lost a game all season.

Before the game, Blaze Head Coach Keaton Warner talked to his team. "Guys, they're the best team in the league. We've got nothing to lose, so I want you to be aggressive out there. Battle for loose balls, and play with some attitude. Let's go!"

The Flyers were a dangerous bunch. They were led by their big center, Robert "Thrasher" Troutman. Thrasher was more than six feet tall and weighed more than 200 pounds. He was their star and leading scorer. But the Flyers also had a solid starting five and a deep bench.

The two teams were warming up. Players on the Blaze tried to get ready for a tough game. Point guard Steve "Steve-O" Lewis practiced a reverse lay-up. Meanwhile, "Q" glanced over at Thrasher. Q, the center of the Blaze, had the job of guarding Thrasher. He turned to Nuno Muandumba, who was practicing his jump shot. "Hey, Nuno, you're our captain—any idea how we stop Thrasher?"

Thirteen-year-old Nuno Muandumba is an intense competitor. He's respected because of his great talent. Nuno offered words of encouragement to Q. Then he glanced over to the Flyers' side of the court, locking eyes with Thrasher. The two captains stared at each other for a moment before turning away. There was mutual respect between them.

For Nuno, this game was the conclusion of a long season . . . and an even longer journey. Sure, he was nervous about being in a packed gym. The season was on the line and everyone was relying on him. But Nuno wouldn't have wanted it any other way. This was exactly where he wanted to be. After all, he had traveled more than 10,000 miles to get here.

From Angola to America

Boom! An explosion ripped through the cool night air. It caused five-year-old Nuno Muandumba to jump up from a deep, peaceful sleep. He swung his legs over the side of the bed and rubbed his tired eyes.

"It's okay, Nuno. It was a couple of blocks away," said his mother. She rushed over to comfort her youngest son.

"Is Dad home yet?" Nuno asked with a worried voice. His father was an important government official. He was away on business.

"Soon, Nuno." She tried to sound confident. "Now, go back to sleep." She tucked him in and watched as he quickly fell back asleep. She didn't want to frighten her son, but she was worried also. Mr. Muandumba had been scheduled to arrive earlier in the day.

Nuno's family lived in Angola, a large country in southern Africa. Unfortunately, it wasn't safe there. A civil war had been tearing the country apart. Rebel troops were a constant danger.

Nuno woke up early the next morning. His mother was busy taking care of his baby sister. Mrs. Muandumba didn't want Nuno to mope around the house worrying about his father. She sent him out with his brother to play. As always, they kicked around a soccer ball for a while. There was also a rusty basketball hoop in a junkyard down the street. Although basketball wasn't popular in Angola, Nuno was interested in the sport.

Several hours later, Nuno and his brother returned home. As they walked through their front door, a big surprise was waiting for them. There, sitting in his favorite armchair, was their father! Nuno and his brother screamed with joy and ran over to him.

This was a time for celebration. Things were about to happen that would change Nuno's life forever. His father hugged him. He said, "Nuno, you are Angolan. Our country and our culture will always be a part of you. But now it's time to pack up your stuff, my son. We're going on a long trip."

Nuno was excited because taking a trip is always fun. But it was actually more than a trip. His parents had decided that it was time for the family to move on. They wanted to go to a country where their children could grow up safely. They had made an important decision. They were moving to America.

All Tied Up

When the game started, Nuno kicked it out to Q, who drained a short jumper. A blocked shot then led to a three-point play for Steve-O. With less than a minute gone, the Blaze had jumped out to a 5-0 lead.

The talented Flyers came right back. Thrasher made his way down low for an easy lay-up. The next time down, he got an offensive rebound put-back and was fouled. A few minutes later, the Flyers hit a long three-pointer from the corner.

The game was extremely tight. Every time the Flyers jumped into the lead, the Blaze stormed back. Nuno had already scored twelve points. He was playing brilliant defense as well. By halftime, the game was right back where it started—all tied up. It was 32-all as both teams headed into the locker room.

The players toweled off and sipped cold water as Coach Warner spoke to them. "Great work, guys, I love what I'm seeing out there. Nobody expected us to play them this tight. Keep working hard out there, don't let up."

Coach Warner's words inspired everyone, especially Nuno. He was a little tired because he hadn't come out of the game. Still, he was on fire. He had dished out five assists already. He was also six for seven from the field. Nuno's accurate shooting touch was very satisfying, because it hadn't *always* been that way. Nuno can still remember the worst shooting night of his life. It was a major turning point for him.

Nightmare

"Oh, man, was I terrible," Nuno says, breaking out into a big smile. He can laugh about it now, but back then there was nothing funny about it.

A year earlier, Nuno and his team had been playing in the spring league. They needed a win to advance to the championship. When the game began, Nuno missed a couple of easy jumpers. He didn't think anything of it. Surely his next shot would go in, or at least the one after that.

Unfortunately, Nuno's next shot missed. And the next. And the next! Before he even knew what happened, Nuno had missed seven shots in a row. At halftime, his team was down by six and Nuno didn't have a single point. He was worried, of course, but he tried to remain upbeat.

The rest of the game was like a nightmare. Nuno's shot refused to drop. The team lost by five points and was knocked out of the tournament. The crowd was shocked, but nobody was more stunned than Nuno. He looked over the stat sheet. "Coach, I was 0 for 14," he said quietly. "I missed every shot I took."

"Maybe so, Nuno, but you didn't cost us the game," Coach Warner responded. "Without you, we would have never even gotten this far. All superstars have bad nights once in a while. Great players learn from these types of things. I know you want to step your game up to the next level. So you need to spend a lot of time in the gym this summer."

Nuno realized that Coach Warner was right. For the next six months, he worked on his jump shot. He also worked on building up leg strength. That way, he wouldn't get tired late in the game. He would still be able to shoot accurately when other players were exhausted.

Nuno was *very* determined to improve. He just kept working harder and harder. Plus, he was growing and getting stronger. He was nearly five feet ten inches. All those extra hours he put in started to pay off. Nuno developed a much better jumpshot. His confidence was at an all-time high. He was ready to become the leader of the Blaze.

Mr. Smooth

As the second half began, Thrasher started scoring at will. Everyone on the Blaze looked to Nuno. He responded like a champion. He was sinking jumpers and setting up his teammates for wide-open shots. Nuno's performance helped keep the score close.

Late in the game, each team was jumping back and forth into the lead. The clock was winding down. Thrasher hit a sweet baseline jumper that touched nothing but net. Then, with a two-point lead, the Flyers forced a turnover. The ball belonged to them with just under ten seconds remaining.

Coach Warner called a quick timeout. The game seemed to be out of reach for the Blaze. "Okay, guys, our only chance is to go for a quick steal. If we don't get it, foul right away. We need the ball back or else we're gonna lose."

As the huddle broke, Nuno looked at his coach with complete confidence. "I won't let us lose, Coach."

With a smile, Coach Warner said, "I know you won't, *Mr. Smooth.*"

Nuno had once attended a basketball clinic at the America West Arena. That's the home of the exciting Phoenix Suns. A former NBA superstar had been on hand to help out with the clinic. His name was Connie Hawkins. The brilliant former pro was best known for his spectacular dunks. He noticed Nuno gliding smoothly to the hoop. Mr. Hawkins was so impressed that he called him "Mr. Smooth." The nickname stuck.

After the timeout, the Flyers inbounded the ball. Their point guard passed it to a teammate near half-court. Nuno saw his opportunity. He darted over and managed to get a finger on the ball. It bounced off the other player's leg, out of bounds. The ref blew his whistle and signaled that it was Blaze ball. But there were no timeouts left and only six seconds remaining!

The ref handed the ball to Q, who spotted Nuno near center court. Q passed it to him. Nuno took one dribble and quickly glanced at the clock—three seconds left. There was no time to drive toward the basket. Making matters worse, another defender had rushed over to help out on him. It was Thrasher! Nuno went up for a jumper. He was at least thirty-five feet out, far beyond the three-point line. Concentrating on the basket, Nuno let the ball fly. The Blaze would win or lose the championship game on this one shot.

As he shot the ball, Nuno fell over backwards. Laying flat on his back, he couldn't even see the ball. But when the final buzzer rang and he heard the loud cheers, he *knew*. Suddenly Coach Warner and his team-mates were happily running toward him.

Nuno's shot had been a perfect swish.

It was a fitting end to a terrific season. "My heart was beating really fast," he remembers. "It was the greatest feeling of my entire life. Even though hard work can be painful, the joy it brings makes it worth it."

Hard work has certainly paid off for Nuno Muandumba. He had to move to a new country when he was a small child. Then he had to find ways to improve himself in the game he loves. This kid has turned himself into an awesome basketball player. Nuno is someone to keep an eye on. He's also a future star of America!

Nuno Muandumba and the Arizona Blaze.

Always Down for Each Other

Now or Never

The clock was winding down in the fourth quarter. The Vikings were trailing the Chiefs 27-20. Making matters worse, their star running back was injured. On the previous play, Rex Sanders had suffered a sprained knee. Watching him limp to the bench in pain, the large crowd fell silent. They realized that the Vikings were facing an uphill battle. Without Rex, getting all the way into the end zone was going to be tough.

Rex was sitting on the bench with an ice pack on his knee. He made eye contact with Coach Jackson. The coach knew exactly what his star player was thinking: *Let me get back in there, Coach. I can play through the pain.*

The Vikings didn't quit, even with Rex out of the game. Eleven-year-old Danny Jenkins was the team's quarterback. He threw a short spiral into the waiting arms of Robbie Baltimore. It was now third down and four.

Over on the sideline, Coach Jackson paused before signaling the next play. If Rex had been in the game, the Vikings would have given him the ball. They would have relied on their best player to pick up the first down. But without Rex, the coach had to call a different play.

Running back Rex Sanders of
Minnesota, poses for the camera.

As the ball was snapped, Rex leaned forward and shouted encouragement. "Come on, Vikings!" he yelled. Danny pitched the ball to Robbie in the backfield. Robbie managed to gain five yards before stepping out of bounds.

"Nice job, Robbie. Way to go!" Rex pumped his fist into the air.

The Vikings had just made it to the Chiefs' forty-five yard line. They still had a chance. Unfortunately, the clock was working against them. It was now or never. Rex removed the ice pack and rolled down his pant leg. He stood up and flexed his knee. Coach Jackson looked at him and barked, "Get in there, Sanders."

Grinning, the 100-pound running back snapped on his helmet and sprinted onto the field. A huge roar went up from the crowd.

"Back in the game at running back, number 41, Rex Sanders!"

A Fiery Competitor

By the time Rex was in first grade, he was already into football. He had a lot of natural talent. His coach made him the team's quarterback. But Rex soon realized that he was born to run, not pass. He switched over to running back. "I just love making plays, running over somebody, or making a nice move to get a first down," Rex explains.

Rex, now thirteen years old, is a fiery competitor. When he decided to take up track a few years ago, he was outstanding. His speedy legs carried him all the way to the Junior Olympics. Another sport Rex likes is lacrosse. One of his best achievements was being selected to the state all-star team.

There's a lot more to Rex Sanders than just sports. He has fun hanging out with his friends, watching movies, and doing things outdoors. Still, he always finds time to do his schoolwork. Rex has an impressive grade point average.

Next year Rex will be starting high school near his home in Apple Valley, Minnesota. He will be testing his football skills against older and more experienced players. This is a challenge that Rex looks forward to. With a wide grin he says, "I'm really excited about high school football. To be the best, you have to play against the best. I'm ready . . . I can't wait!"

Important Decision

Rex didn't waste any time once he got back into the game. On the very first play, he exploded up the middle for a twelve-yard gain. The crowd rose to its feet. After an incomplete pass, Danny handed the ball to Rex again. The Chiefs were ready, meeting him at the line of scrimmage. Rex had run into a wall of defenders. Still, he displayed his strength by pushing his way forward. He managed to gain four yards.

It was now third down and six with less than a minute remaining. Danny pitched it to Rex, who ran for a gain of nine yards. Rex had picked up another first down for his team. The Vikings were on the twenty yard line with just thirty-two seconds left to play.

Next, the Vikings ran "orange-blue." This play called for Danny to fake a slant pass to Robbie. Instead, he would throw a sideline pass to Rex. It worked perfectly. Rex jumped in the air and caught the ball for a pick-up of eleven yards. The official marked the ball at the nine yard line—first and goal.

With the crowd screaming, Rex picked up six yards on the next play. He wisely stepped out of bounds, stopping the clock with only fifteen seconds left. The Vikings were now on the Chiefs' three yard line! Danny looked over at Coach Jackson for the play. The coach gave a hand signal. Nodding his head, Danny made his way over to the huddle. "D-coy 1," he said simply.

Rex didn't say anything, but he was a little surprised. So was everyone else in the huddle. D-coy 1 meant that Rex would not touch the ball. Danny would fake it to him but hand it off to the fullback, Corey Williams. The coach had made an important decision. The Vikings had been going to Rex on almost every play. He felt that Rex might be a little tired. Also, he was sure that the defense wasn't expecting D-coy 1.

As they lined up, Corey Williams looked nervous. "Hike!" Danny yelled. He took the snap and faked a handoff to Rex, who ran toward the sideline. The defense followed Rex. They were completely fooled when Danny gave the ball to Corey. Unfortunately, Corey wasn't able to take advantage. A step slow, he was met at the line of scrimmage and stopped cold. It was now third and goal.

Danny called timeout and ran over to the sideline. The coach told him to run the same play. It produced only one yard. The Vikings called their final timeout. It was fourth down with only three seconds left to play. They *had* to score. They were on the two yard line! Everyone figured that this time the ball would definitely be going to Rex. But it wasn't. The coach was still certain that D-coy 1 was the right call. So he sent Danny back to the huddle to set it up.

"Hike!" For the very last time, Danny faked the handoff to Rex. Once again he gave the ball to Corey. The fullback stumbled, losing his balance. Corey didn't gain a single yard.

The game was over.

"Just Between us Players"

There was a stunned silence as the final buzzer sounded. The Chiefs were jumping up and down, celebrating the victory. Slowly, the Vikings started leaving the field. But not Rex. He was angry, upset, and disappointed. He went over and sat down by himself at the fifty yard line.

"Mind a little company?" Rex looked up and saw his grandfather. Rex was a little embarrassed because some tears had run down his cheeks. His grandfather smiled gently.

"Rex, just between us football players, I'll let you in on a little secret: I've shed those very same tears myself on many occasions."

Rex has never doubted where his talent for football comes from. His grandfather, Dave Osborn, is a former NFL player. He played in the 1960s and 1970s with the hometown Minnesota Vikings.

Rex wiped a tear away. "Yeah, but this must seem pretty stupid to you after some of the pressure playoff games you played in the NFL."

"Stupid?" Mr. Osborn put his hand around his grandson's shoulders. "Let me tell you something, Rex: there's *never* anything stupid about trying as hard as you can, or caring about winning as much as you do. Those are qualities I admire in you. I would have been proud to call you a teammate."

Hearing words of praise from his grandfather made Rex feel better. He sat up and said, "Grandpa, I kept waiting to get the play called for me. But Coach went to Corey instead. I could have made it into the end zone, I just *know* it."

Mr. Osborn smiled. "I have no doubt about it, Rex. But there's something even more important than the outcome of the game. Unfortunately, Corey wasn't able to get the job done. Can you imagine how he's feeling right now?"

The expression on Rex's face changed completely. He had been focused on his own disappointment. "You're right, Grandpa," Rex said. "He must think he let the team down and that's why we lost. It wasn't his fault, though. You've always taught me that a team wins together *and* loses together."

"I'll bet Corey could use that kind of support right now," the former NFL star said softly.

Rex stood up and gave his grandfather a hug. He ran to catch up with the rest of the Vikings. When he reached the locker room, he walked right over to Corey. Speaking loudly, Rex said, "Dude, good try out there. Today wasn't our day, but you know what? We're a team, and we win and lose as a team. When we walk out of here, let's hold our heads high. We're still the Vikings, and we're *always down for each other*—no matter what."

When Rex saw a big smile spread across Corey's face, he felt fantastic. Rex was grateful for his grandfather's help. Mr. Osborn has always been there for Rex. He's never missed one of his games. Rex definitely wants to follow in his grandfather's foot-steps. He wants to do some of the things he has done—like play in *four* NFL Super Bowls!

Success

Two weeks after the Vikings lost to the Chiefs, the teams played again. The Vikings needed a win to get back in first place. The contest was only ten min-utes old, but they had just fallen behind, 7-0.

As usual, Rex lined up near his end zone to

return the kickoff. He ran under it and made the catch. Rex got past the first two defenders easily. Then he crashed right into another defender. He spun around him before breaking free up the sideline. Cutting back to his left, Rex found himself sprinting down the middle of the field. There was only one defender to beat. The defender, Jimmy Watkins, was the Chiefs' best player. At 125 pounds, he was the biggest and strongest kid on the field.

Jimmy raced across the field to get at Rex. This was going to be a very hard hit! But something happened just before they collided. A body came flying out of nowhere to lay a fantastic block on Jimmy. The crunching sound could be heard up in the top row of the bleachers. Rex never saw who saved the day for him. He was too busy running into the end zone for a touchdown.

As soon as Rex crossed the goal line, he turned around. He wanted to know who had made the amazing block. When he saw that it was Corey Williams, he smiled. Ripping off his helmet, he ran toward Corey. Rex said, "Dude, Corey, you saved me."

"That was my way of saying thanks, Rex, for sticking up for me after I messed up that other game," Corey said. The two teammates started walking happily toward the sideline together. Rex looked into the stands, where his grandfather was staring at him proudly. At that moment, Rex realized something important. The lessons his grandfather teaches him are

Rex and his grandfather, former Minnesota Viking, Dave Osborn, after a game.

helping him become a better football player. They're also helping him become a better person.

Rex Sanders has a great family guiding him in the right direction. He wrote a paper in English class that shows the kind of guy he is. Part of Rex's essay said: "Success is trying your best and having fun doing it. It's about achieving goals that you always dreamed of. Success is also about being the kind of person who does cool things. Even something small—

like sitting next to a kid who doesn't have anyone to sit with at lunch."

Rex is qualified to talk about success. Sure, being a football player is in his blood. But what really stands out is his character. He strikes a balance between sports and all other parts of his life. Rex may get the chance to play in the Super Bowl like his grandfather. But even if he doesn't, Rex Sanders is a super success . . . and a future star of America!